MODERN ROLE MODELS

Dwayne "The Rock" Johnson

James A. Corrick

Mason Crest Publishers

Produced by OTTN Publishing in association with
21st Century Publishing and Communications, Inc.

MASON CREST PUBLISHERS INC.
370 Reed Road
Broomall, Pennsylvania 19008
(866) MCP-BOOK (toll free)
www.masoncrest.com

Printed in the United States of America.

First Printing

9 8 7 6 5 4 3 2

Library of Congress Cataloging-in-Publication Data

Corrick, James A.
  Dwayne "The Rock" Johnson / James A. Corrick.
    p. cm. — (Modern role models)
  ISBN 978-1-4222-0503-7 (hardcover) — ISBN 978-1-4222-0790-1 (pbk.)
  1. Rock (Wrestler)—Juvenile literature 2. Wrestlers—United States—
Biography—Juvenile literature. I. Title.
GV1196.R63C67 2009
796.812092—dc22
[B]   2008025063

Publisher's note:
All quotations in this book come from original sources, and contain the spelling and grammatical inconsistencies of the original text.

CROSS-CURRENTS

In the ebb and flow of the currents of life we are each influenced by many people, places, and events that we directly experience or have learned about. Throughout the chapters of this book you will come across CROSS-CURRENTS reference boxes. These boxes direct you to a CROSS-CURRENTS section in the back of the book that contains fascinating and informative sidebars and related pictures. Go on. ▸▸

CONTENTS

As a professional wrestler, Dwayne "The Rock" Johnson was known for being tough on opponents in the ring. But in real life Dwayne is very different from his wrestling persona. Over the years he has made an effort to give back to people in need. Dwayne is especially involved with charities that help young children.

1

The Rock Has Heart

DURING HIS YEARS WITH WORLD WRESTLING Entertainment (WWE), Dwayne "The Rock" Johnson was one of the superstars of professional wrestling. The Rock was colorful, dynamic, and just plain fun to watch. He was also fun to listen to as he tore into his opponents with words as well as deeds.

In his years as a professional wrestler, the Rock made an unforgettable mark on the industry. He was the first African American to win the WWE Championship. He held the title a record seven times. He also held the WWE Intercontinental Championship title twice and the World Tag Team Championship title five times. The Rock's success and popularity earned him the title the People's Champion. He was the champion who always played to the fans. He was the champion that wrestling audiences wanted to see and to cheer on. Thomas Chamberlin wrote in a December 2000 *Wrestling Digest* article:

> **By the beginning of 2000, the Rock was drawing sell-out crowds by himself. He was beginning to become a mainstream celebrity. His autobiography ('*The Rock Says . . .*') was on top of *The New York Times* best-seller list. The line was long for a chance to grab The Rock for appearances and interviews.**

Since ending his wrestling career in 2004, Dwayne has put his energy into his film career. By the time he retired from wrestling, he already had a number of successful movies behind him, including *The Scorpion King* (2002) and *Walking Tall* (2004). He is primarily an action star, although he has moved into comedy with his recent films *The Game Plan* (2007) and *Get Smart* (2008).

THE ROCK GIVES BACK

As the Rock, Dwayne Johnson came across as an all-around tough guy. However, Dwayne has a heart, and he knows when and how to reach out a helping hand to others. He uses his reputation and the money he has earned to aid others in need. Indeed, in 2007 the Giving Back Fund listed Dwayne and his wife, Dany Garcia Johnson, as among the 30 most generous celebrities with their time and money.

Dwayne is particularly interested in the needs of children. He is a national spokesperson for After-School All-Stars. This organization sponsors activities and programs after the school day ends in areas that have no such programs. Dwayne also takes part in the Make-A-Wish Foundation program, which grants the wishes of seriously ill and dying children. In 2006 no celebrity received more requests from children through the Make-A-Wish Foundation than the Rock.

THE ROCK FOUNDATION

Besides working with Make-A-Wish, Dwayne and Dany also set up the DJ Rock Foundation in September 2006. The foundation has several goals. These include: bettering the lives of hospitalized children due to serious illness or disability; improving the health and self-esteem of children through exercise programs such as the Children's Fitness Challenge; and educating kids on eating right and other healthy practices. The foundation's mission is to lend a helping hand to children in need around the world and of all ages, from infancy to 22 years of age. The foundation posts this message on its Web site:

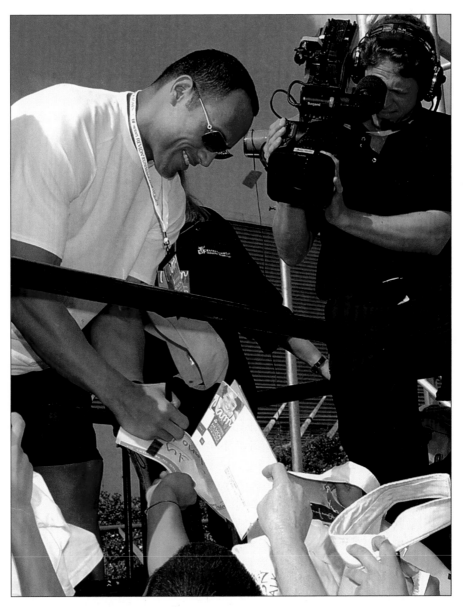

Dwayne Johnson signs autographs at an event to benefit the UCLA Women's Cancer Research Program in Los Angeles. Although Dwayne's popularity means that he is in great demand, he always makes time to help worthwhile causes. Dwayne has been involved with the Make-A-Wish Foundation, the Rush Philanthropic Arts Foundation, and Until There's a Cure, which educates young people about AIDS.

CROSS-CURRENTS

To find out about how the Rock has helped to promote healthier young people, read "Children's Fitness Challenge." Go to page 48. ▶▶

"Our staff and board of directors, comprised of experienced philanthropists and entertainment professionals, believe in the potential of children and the importance of a nurturing, positive and supportive environment for them to recover, learn and grow.**"**

THE ROCK'S TOY CHESTS

One of the foundation's most successful programs is the Rock's Toy Chest. Each toy chest is actually a large playhouse. It is shaped like a fort and is located in a hospital's playroom or recreation area. The fort is filled with toys for sick or disabled children who must stay in the hospital for a long time. Each hospital containing a toy chest has around 60 young patients.

In order to collect the most-desired toys, the Rock Foundation works with hospital staff members to find out what toys their young patients want. Every three months, the foundation adds new toys to a hospital's chest. So far, Rock Toy Chests are found in the hospitals of three major U.S. cities—Boston, Los Angeles, and Miami (the Rock's home). The foundation expects to have toy chests in other cities in the future.

Another special program of the Rock Foundation is the Rock's Global Toy Chest. In this program, a 40-foot-long box is sent to children in need in Latin America, Asia, and Africa. Among the countries receiving these shipments are El Salvador, Guatemala, Cambodia, and Zimbabwe. The chests contain articles such as clothing, soccer balls, sneakers, and even cameras. They may have pens and pencils, crayons, notebooks, construction paper, and other school supplies. Toys like building blocks and Lincoln Logs are also sent by the foundation.

BUILDING FOR THE FUTURE

Dwayne not only lends his nickname to the foundation, but he is also chairman of its board of directors. Fundraising is important to him, and at the opening of his 2006 film *The Gridiron Gang*, he asked audience members to bring toys for the Rock's Toy Chest.

Dwayne visits with two kids at the Miami Science Museum in September 2007. He attended an event at the museum to accept a donation of toys for hospitalized children. Over the years Dwayne and Dany Johnson have given toys to children in hospitals through their charitable organization, the DJ Rock Foundation.

Dany also plays an active role in the organization. She is a former vice president of the investment firm Merrill Lynch and is currently the chief executive officer (CEO) of a wealth management firm. She brings her business experience to the Rock Foundation, serving as its CEO.

Dwayne Johnson has shown that beneath his tough exterior, he has a good heart. It is that quality that endears him to millions of fans and makes him a modern role model for many young people.

Wearing a colorful shirt, young Dwayne poses with his parents, Rocky and Ata Johnson. A photo of Rocky wearing a championship belt hangs on the wall behind the family. As the son and grandson of professional wrestlers, Dwayne became familiar with the business of pro wrestling at an early age.

Before the Rock

DWAYNE DOUGLAS JOHNSON WAS BORN MAY 2, 1972, in Hayward, California, to Rocky and Ata Johnson. Rocky was an ex-boxer and one of the first successful African American professional wrestlers. Ata's family came from the South Pacific island group of Samoa. Her father, Peter Maivia, was also a professional wrestler.

⇒ MOVING AROUND ⇐

Because of Rocky Johnson's career, the family moved often. The family even moved to New Zealand for a time. Eventually, Dwayne's family settled in Hawaii. Ata's parents also lived in Hawaii, and Dwayne got to know his grandfather. From Peter Maivia, Dwayne learned about Samoan culture.

Throughout all of these moves, wrestling became a constant for the young Dwayne. He sometimes went with his mother to see his

CROSS-CURRENTS

For more information about the history and culture of Dwayne's mother's home country, read "Samoa." Go to page 49. ▶▶

father's matches. As a young boy, he practiced wrestling moves. Later, he wrote in his autobiography:

> **"I was fascinated by the business. I loved everything about it: the violence, the theatricality, the athleticism, the volume . . . *everything*! By the time I was six years old I was practicing dropkicks and head locks on our dog. By the time I was eight I was trying to have serious discussions about the business with my father. "**

From the beginning, Dwayne was aware that professional wrestling matches were scripted and that wrestlers were actors. The wrestler's job was to put on the best and most entertaining show possible. A good wrestler was a good performer, and Dwayne knew his father was one of the best.

⇒ PLAYING FOOTBALL ⇐

Dwayne's interest in wrestling, however, did not keep him from other sports. In high school he played football. By 1988, Dwayne's junior year, his family was living in Bethlehem, Pennsylvania, and he was attending Bethlehem Freedom High School. That year, he was one of the football team's captains and also was named to the all-conference team. In his senior year, college football programs began trying to recruit him.

In spite of these achievements, Dwayne had not given up his desire to be a pro wrestler Yet, for the moment, football seemed more exciting and more promising. According to his autobiography, Dwayne hoped that one day he would play in the National Football League (NFL).

⇒ THE UNIVERSITY OF MIAMI ⇐

In 1990 Dwayne entered the University of Miami. There, he played defensive tackle for the Miami Hurricanes and was part of the 1991 national championship team. However, several injuries limited his ability to play. Dwayne became depressed because of his injuries and almost failed school. But he soon pulled himself out of his depression and buckled down to his studies. In 1995 he graduated with a degree in **criminology**.

Dwayne in a University of Miami Hurricanes uniform. Dwayne was part of a Hurricanes football squad that went 12-0 and won the national championship in 1991. Dwayne remained on Miami's football team for the next three seasons. However, a back injury before his senior year probably ruined his chances of playing in the NFL.

During his freshman year at Miami, Dwayne had met Dany Garcia. She quickly became his girlfriend. In 1993 they moved in together and lived together off and on for the next several years.

THE END OF FOOTBALL

Dwayne's dreams of playing for the NFL did not come true. He was not offered a contract with any NFL team. Instead, in 1995, he went to Canada to play for the Calgary Stampeders of the Canadian Football League. However, after only a few months, Calgary dropped him. Everyone agreed that Dwayne was a good football player, but so were a lot of other players, and there were only a limited number of spots on any team.

In the fall of 1995 Dwayne arrived back in Miami, broke and jobless. It was the lowest point in his life. But he did not give in to despair. Instead, he decided to drop football and seek a career in professional wrestling, his first love.

TURNING PRO

Dwayne asked his father to train him. At first, Rocky refused. He felt that Dwayne should continue pursuing his football career. However, Dwayne's determination to become a pro wrestler convinced Rocky to begin training his son. Within a few months Dwayne was ready to try out for a spot in World Wrestling Entertainment (WWE), a major promoter and organizer of professional wrestling. He had his tryout match in Corpus Christi, Texas, and impressed the WWE.

CROSS-CURRENTS

To learn more about the life and wrestling career of Dwayne's father, check out "Rocky Johnson." Go to page 50. ▶▶

In May 1996 Dwayne signed a contract with the WWE. To sharpen his skills, he was sent to Memphis, Tennessee. There, the WWE sponsored regional matches featuring young, unknown wrestlers. If Dwayne did well in Memphis, he would be promoted to wrestling in national WWE matches.

Fighting under the name Flex Kavana, Dwayne found himself wrestling in all sorts of places, among them car dealership parking lots and barns. He did well, and in September 1996 the WWE told him to report to WWE headquarters in Stamford, Connecticut.

ROCKY MAIVIA, STAR

The WWE decided to rename Dwayne, and he became Rocky Maivia. The WWE thought this name built upon the reputations of both Dwayne's father and grandfather.

The WWE then cast Rocky Maivia as a **babyface**, or hero. In November 1996 he wrestled in his first WWE match at Madison

Square Garden in New York City. This match was a Survivor Series event and was extremely popular. Winners of such events were the stars of the WWE. Vince McMahon, chairman of the WWE, and other top WWE officers thought Dwayne could be one of those stars. They selected Rocky Maivia to win the 1996 Survivor Series. In his book, *The Rock Says . . .*, Dwayne writes:

> **"When Rocky Maivia won the *Survivor Series* in his World Wrestling Entertainment debut, the fans knew they were looking at a guy who was going to be around for a while."**

And indeed he would be.

Dwayne in costume as Rocky Maivia during a World Wrestling Entertainment match. Rocky made an immediate impact on the WWE, winning his first event, the Survivor Series in Madison Square Garden. He soon became the youngest wrestler to win a WWE championship. However, fans did not care for Rocky Maivia's clean-cut image.

Becoming
the Rock

AFTER THE SURVIVOR SERIES, ROCKY MAIVIA
continued to climb the WWE's ranks. In February 1997
the WWE selected him to take the Intercontinental
Championship title from the wrestler Hunter Hearst
Helmsley. It was Rocky's first WWE championship win.
It made him one of the youngest WWE champions of all
time. The WWE saw star potential in their new wrestler.

The WWE also continued to promote Rocky Maivia as a third-
generation wrestler and kept publicly linking him with his famous
father and grandfather. This did not mean that Dwayne coasted on
his family's reputation. He worked hard to be the best performer and
wrestler that he could be.

⇒ ROCKY MAIVIA AND THE FANS ⇐

The fans were less thrilled with Rocky Maivia than the WWE was.
Dwayne's character was a babyface, a hero, and wrestling audiences

CROSS-CURRENTS

To find out more about pro wrestling's good guys and bad guys, read "Babyfaces and Heels." Go to page 51. ▶▶

were supposed to root for him against his opponent. The opponent was a **heel**, or a villain. As a babyface Rocky Maivia smiled a lot and fought by the rules. Sometimes he won, and sometimes the heel used some dirty trick to defeat him.

Audiences, however, began to shout insults at Rocky and to treat him more like a heel than a babyface. The fans did not like him. His character was too old-fashioned for them, too boring.

⇒ GETTING MARRIED ⇐

Dwayne's wrestling career might have hit a snag, but not his personal life. He and Dany decided to marry in the spring of 1997. The only problem was Dany's parents. Dwayne and Dany had been together for almost six years, but her parents had refused to meet Dwayne. They did not approve of him. In a 2001 interview with Zondra Hughes for *Ebony*, Dwayne explained:

> **❝**Her parents were Cuban immigrants who were adamant about being American. . . . English was always their first language in their home. They wanted their children to assimilate, adapt and succeed. What they did not want was their daughter dating me, a person of color. I was half-Black, and that made me an unsuitable suitor.**❞**

Days before the wedding, Dwayne and Dany made a surprise visit to her parents. The visit was awkward, but the news of the marriage impressed the Garcias. They realized how committed Dwayne and Dany were to each other. The two were married with both of their families present on May 3, 1997.

⇒ TURNING HEEL ⇐

Meanwhile, the WWE was listening to the fans. In the summer of 1997, the WWE's higher-ups changed Dwayne from a babyface to a heel. He then joined the **tag team** Nation of Dominance, a heel group. Wrestling fans loved Rocky's heel turn. They also loved the fact that in interviews, called **promos**, he began insulting them. Rocky had become a wrestler the fans loved to hate.

Dany and Dwayne Johnson arrive at the premiere of *Doom*, a 2005 film in which Dwayne had a leading role. Dany has said that beneath his tough-guy image, Dwayne is a softie. "He is the kind of guy who'll sing to me when I'm not feeling well," she said in a 1999 interview. "He notices that you've changed your hair."

Dwayne continued wrestling as Rocky Maivia until December 1997. Then the WWE decided to pit him against its reigning superstar, Stone Cold Steve Austin. The WWE also decided that Dwayne needed a stronger, more forceful name. This is when he became the Rock.

⟫ THE ROCK ⟪

From the beginning Dwayne had a clear picture of who the Rock was. He wrote in his autobiography:

> **"**I saw The Rock as an extension of my own personality. He was . . . cocky, funny, but at his core, he was an athlete with sound technical skills. He loved wrestling. He loved sports-entertainment. The Rock was Dwayne Johnson . . . with the volume . . . turned . . . WAY . . . UP!**"**

And indeed, the Rock was larger than life. He admitted to no failings. He was constantly boastful and completely self-centered, always referring to himself in the third person. He did not care what others thought of him.

⟫ THE ROCK'S MOVES ⟪

The Rock used standard wrestling moves such as the **leg drop** and the **body slam**. He also had a number of **signature moves** that only he used. The Rock's two most famous signature moves were the Rock Bottom and the People's Elbow. The Rock Bottom was a form of body slam. The Rock and his opponent would stand side by side. The Rock would hook his opponent's head and neck with one arm. He would then lift his opponent, while at the same time kick the other wrestler's legs out from under him. Finally, the Rock slammed his opponent onto the mat so that he landed with a crash on his upper body and the back of his head. In 1998, in honor of the Rock, the WWE named one of its events the Rock Bottom.

The Rock's other signature move, the People's Elbow, began with the Rock standing over a fallen wrestler and spinning in a circle. At the same time he pulled off his left elbow pad and threw it into the audience. Then, completing his circle, he dropped elbow first onto his opponent. Sometimes the Rock repeated the move with his right elbow.

The People's Eyebrow was another fan favorite. The Rock would raise one of his eyebrows high. When he did that, fans knew it was a sign he did not take his opponent seriously.

⇒ THE ROCK TALKS ⇐

Of all his trademarks, the Rock's many sayings, or catchphrases, were probably the most popular with the fans. These sayings were always

The Rock (right) slams an opponent to the mat using his signature move, the Rock Bottom. As the Rock, Dwayne played a tough, loud character. He often insulted wrestling fans, as well as his opponents. But even though the Rock was a heel—a bad guy—he soon became an audience favorite.

colorful, and the Rock coined most of them in his promos. The fans considered the promos among the best in the business.

Two of the Rock's most common and most popular catchphrases were, "Do you smell what the Rock is cooking?" and "Layeth the smacketh down." The first question asked the crowd if they understood what the Rock was saying. The second phrase said that the Rock planned to win that night. "Layeth the smacketh down" eventually became the name of a WWE series.

THE ROCK AND THE FANS

The Rock always used the word *jabroni* when referring to his opponents. This was an old pro wrestling term for someone who is a fool or unskilled. He also hurled this insult at the audience. As always with the Rock, the fans loved to be the target of his insults.

In reality, Dwayne Johnson loved the fans. He believed that it was their passion for pro wrestling that created his success. In return for their support, Dwayne as the Rock always gave a first-rate performance. His goal was to entertain. In a 2002 interview with Scott B. Smith of IGN.com, Dwayne said:

> **There's nothing like working in front of a live audience of twenty-thousand passionate, vocal, loyal fans. At the end of the day, they know that I just want to entertain you. Thoroughly entertain you.**

FEUDING

In wrestling, one of the greatest sources of entertainment is the feud. The feud provides much of the drama in WWE storylines. A feud can involve a babyface and a heel, two heels, or teams of wrestlers. The victor sometimes wins by overcoming great odds or through cheating.

December 1997 saw the beginning of one of the WWE's most famous feuds, between the Rock and Stone Cold Steve Austin. The bout with Stone Cold left the Rock with his second Intercontinental Championship title. The two would meet in many more matches, and their feud became legendary. It only added to the popularity of the Rock.

CROSS-CURRENTS
To learn more about the life and career of one of the Rock's greatest rivals, read "Stone Cold Steve Austin." Go to page 52.

The Rock also continued to fight with the Nation of Dominance. The WWE decided to take advantage of his increasing popularity with the fans and created a new storyline for him, involving another feud. This time the object of the feud was Faarooq. Faarooq was the leader of the Nation of Dominance and a major WWE heel. The feud ended in May 1998 with the Rock defeating Faarooq and taking over leadership of the group.

⇒ D-GENERATION X ⇐

Under the Rock's leadership, the Nation of Dominance became simply the Nation. Over the next several months, the Nation's members helped the Rock keep his Intercontinental Championship title.

In helping the Rock, the Nation became involved in a hot feud with another heel tag team, D-Generation X. D-Generation's members were rebels, and their target was any authority figure. D-Generation X was famous for its pranks and jokes. One of its most successful was a takeoff on the Nation. The Rock's D-Generation X counterpart was the Crock.

The Nation was normally the victor in matches with D-Generation X. In the best heel tradition, sometimes the Nation won by cheating, as when they cornered most of D-Generation X in the locker room with a **forklift.**

The leader of D-Generation X was Triple H. He and the Rock had a personal feud inside the larger group feud. The object of the feud was the Intercontinental Championship title. The Rock managed to hold onto the title through several bouts, but in August 1998 at SummerSlam, he finally lost the title to Triple H in a **ladder match**.

⇒ THE WORLD CHAMPION ⇐

The Rock might have lost the Intercontinental Championship title, but he did not lose the favor of the fans. By now, he was such a fan favorite that he was a babyface, not a heel. This increasing popularity led to the Rock's leaving the Nation but not before he had a feud with Mark Henry, one of the Nation's members.

In November 1998 the Rock met Mankind at the Survivor Series in a battle for the WWE World Championship title. Mankind was a heel, and his gimmick was that he wore a leather mask and torn clothes, lived in a boiler room, and had a pet rat. He was a creepy character but nonetheless popular with the crowd.

DWAYNE "THE ROCK" JOHNSON

The leader of D-Generation X, Triple H, strikes an intimidating pose in this publicity photo. His success inside the ring is indisputable: among modern-day wrestlers, no one has reigned as WWE champion for a greater total time than Triple H. During his career, the Rock engaged in heated rivalries with several top wrestlers, including Triple H, Faarooq, and Stone Cold Steve Austin.

In the end the Rock won the World Championship. At 26, he was the youngest wrestler to hold the title up to that time.

⇒ ANOTHER TURN ⇐

The WWE now had a surprise for the fans. At the end of the match with Mankind, the Rock joined a tag team, the Corporation. The leader of the team was Mr. McMahon, one of the most popular heels in wrestling. Mr. McMahon was actually Vince McMahon, the WWE chairman. The other member of the Corporation was McMahon's son Sean, another heel.

The Rock had once more turned heel. It was a turn that the fans would enjoy as he once more came face-to-face with his rival Stone Cold Steve Austin in the months to come.

The Rock raises an eyebrow, one of the gimmicks that made him well known. By 1999 the Rock had become one of the biggest stars of professional wrestling. His sneers and insults drew cheers from audiences. Because of his popularity, Dwayne started to receive offers to appear in movies and on television shows that were not related to wrestling.

The Rock Wrestles and Acts

BY THE BEGINNING OF 1999 THE ROCK HAD become one of World Wrestling Entertainment's superstars. To many fans, he was *the* wrestling superstar. His dynamic promos, his colorful language, and his athletic performances were top entertainment draws for the WWE. It did not matter whether he was a heel or a babyface. Fans could not get enough of the Rock.

⟫ CREATING AN IMAGE ⟪

Dwayne Johnson saw himself as an all-around professional performer and entertainer. He prided himself on always giving the fans the best show possible. In a 2008 interview with Grant Rollings of the British newspaper the *Sun*, Dwayne observed:

> **"You know the outcome of the matches, it's a scripted television show. What I tell guys interested**

CROSS-CURRENTS

To learn more about how professional wrestling matches are meant to be entertainment, read "Wrestling as Theater." Go to page 54. ▶▶

in getting into wrestling is you need to find a way to connect with the live audience. And you don't do that through your biceps. 🙶

Every feature of the Rock was important, including his clothes. Personally, Dwayne favored shorts, T-shirts, and basketball shoes. But when he was playing the Rock outside the ring, he appeared in expensive tailored clothes. His shirts cost up to $500 and a pair of shoes $400. It was all part of the Rock's larger-than-life image.

⇒ THE PROMOS ⇐

Dwayne also put a lot of thought into the Rock's promos. He often woke in the middle of the night and grabbed a notepad and pencil to jot down ideas. In restaurants he wrote notes to himself on napkins. Then Dwayne would sit down with a WWE writer and work out the final promo. In 2002 on *Larry King Live*, Dwayne told King:

🙶We'll sit down and we'll go over . . . what we're going to go over that night. And say, well, let's try this, or let's try that, let's omit this, and let's try this. . . . Not only do I want to be great in the ring, but I want to do my best to raise the bar—continue to raise the bar, in terms of promos. 🙶

⇒ WORKING OUT THE MOVES ⇐

Dwayne also worked closely with other wrestlers on the script. He met with his opponents before a match, and like dancers, they would **choreograph** their moves in the ring. Then they practiced. This was necessary to make the combat look real. Pulling punches and still making them look real was not easy, especially in front of a live audience. Dwayne had spent hours in front of a mirror working on his punching.

This does not mean that wrestlers do not sometimes get hurt. The props pro wrestlers use, unlike those in the movies, are real—real metal chairs and real ladders, for instance. In 1997, while still Rocky Maivia, Dwayne had been out for three months with an

Professional wrestlers must be in good condition so they can perform challenging and dangerous stunts in the ring. Props such as ladders and chairs increase the chances that a wrestler will get hurt. Before his matches, Dwayne worked out each of his moves. He then practiced for many hours to make sure everything turned out all right.

injured knee. Steve Austin eventually had to stop wrestling full-time because of his many injuries.

There was another important key to Dwayne's success as the Rock. He learned his role for each bout and played it as written. But, win or lose, the Rock always did it with zest.

⟫ THE BATTLE FOR THE CHAMPIONSHIP ⟪

January and February 1999 saw the continuation of the Rock and Mankind storyline. The two wrestlers met in a series of matches to fight for the WWE World Championship title.

The main event on January 4 at the WWE event RAW was the Rock defending his title. In the end Mankind won the match and the title with the help of Stone Cold Steve Austin. Together, the two pinned the Rock to the mat.

Three weeks later, the Rock beat Mankind at Royal Rumble 1999 to reclaim the title. In true heel fashion, the Rock knocked Mankind out with a chair and then played a tape recording with Mankind's voice saying, "I quit," to fool the referee into ending the match.

A week later, on January 31, the Rock and Mankind staged a bout during halftime at the Super Bowl. The fight moved all over the stadium and involved throwing popcorn and fruit. At one point, Mankind had a phone cord wrapped around his neck. Mankind finally defeated the Rock, though, by pinning him down with a forklift.

The final chapter of the Rock-Mankind story was on the February 24 RAW. In a ladder match, the Rock won the World Championship title back.

⪻ WRESTLEMANIA 15 ⪼

The Rock's final victory over Mankind set the stage for a renewal of his feud with Stone Cold Steve Austin. On March 28, 1999, the Rock and Stone Cold were the main act at WrestleMania 15. At stake was the World Championship.

The bout lasted some 40 minutes. In that time the two wrestlers scrapped, punched, kicked, and threw each other around inside and outside the ring. In *The Rock Says . . .*, Dwayne writes as the Rock describing the match:

CROSS-CURRENTS

For an in-depth look at the practice required before a championship wrestling event, read "The Rock Prepares for a Match." Go to page 55. ▶▶

❝Austin is getting the better of The Rock. But Austin doesn't understand the immensity of the athlete he's facing. He gets sloppy, and now The Rock is there to greet him with the Rock Bottom . . . WHAM! Right in the middle of the ring! . . . Ohhhhhh! Stone Cold Steve Austin does the impossible—he kicks out of the Rock Bottom. No one has ever done that before.❞

Stone Cold Steve Austin celebrates a victory. The feud between the Rock and Stone Cold was very popular among WWE audiences. Both Stone Cold and the Rock won important matches during the rivalry. In Austin's final WWE match, at Wrestlemania 19 in Seattle on March 30, 2003, he was pinned by the Rock.

Later, the Rock fought his way free of Stone Cold's signature move, the Stone Cold Stunner.

The bout continued with chairs flying, referees being knocked senseless, and Mr. McMahon rushing in to help the Rock. In the end, however, the Rock lost both the match and the World Championship title.

WrestleMania 15 sold more tickets than any other WWE event up until that time, and it did so chiefly because of the matchup of the Rock and Stone Cold. Reviews of the bout later rated it as one of the greatest pro wrestling shows ever. And indeed, Dwayne Johnson believed it was perhaps his best performance.

⇒ LIFE OUTSIDE THE RING ⇐

Dwayne always enjoyed the pro wrestling business, in large part because of the passion of his fans. Still, at times the life could be a lonely one. Dwayne had to spend much of the year traveling around the United States to different WWE events. Dany had a good job as a financial consultant in Miami, so she could not join him on the road. The two were often apart for long stretches.

At home, Dwayne and Dany lived a quiet life. Dwayne worked out to stay in shape, and for fun was an avid saltwater fisherman. His fame sometimes made shopping a challenge, though. He and Dany shopped early in the day or late in the evening. At these times there were fewer shoppers and less likelihood of attracting the attention of wrestling fans. Dwayne was always willing to sign autographs, but a crowd of admirers could make buying groceries or other items difficult. Such crowds could also annoy other shoppers.

On the road and outside the ring, Dwayne's life was also quiet. He rarely went out and rarely drank alcohol. Instead, he preferred to return alone to his hotel room after a match and watch a movie as he drank bottled water.

⇒ THE ROCK ROCKS ON ⇐

In the ring, the Rock left The Corporation soon after WrestleMania 15 and began feuds with both of the McMahons, Triple H, and the Undertaker. He had once more turned and was now a babyface. The Rock sometimes found himself fighting side by side with his old rival, Stone Cold Steve Austin. WWE storylines often called for such odd partnerships to keep audiences surprised.

Mankind had also turned babyface, and he and the Rock teamed up in what was called the Rock 'N' Sock Connection. As a member of this tag team, the Rock won the first of his five World Tag Team Championships. Fans found the Rock 'N' Sock Connection very entertaining, and it became one of the most popular wrestling teams of all time. Many claimed the highlight was the "This Is Your Life" program. In this program Mankind brought out people from the Rock's past. The fans enjoyed seeing The Rock's high school girl-friend and gym teacher, and the program was one of the most watched WWE events ever.

EXPANDING TO OTHER AREAS

While Dwayne enjoyed his success, he knew that professional wrestling was a hard business physically. Most wrestlers were finished by their forties. His own father had retired at age 47. This reality led Dwayne to branch out into television. He appeared in episodes of *The Net* and *That '70s Show*. On *That '70s Show* he played his father, Rocky Johnson. The next year, 2000, he had a role in a *Star Trek: Voyager* episode and hosted *Saturday Night Live*. In all of these shows Dwayne billed himself as the Rock.

The *Saturday Night Live* hosting brought him to the attention of several film producers, and he began to receive offers for film roles. He hoped to follow other wrestlers such as Hulk Hogan into the movies.

In August 2000 the Rock took on another role. He joined other celebrities at the Republican National Convention. Here, he introduced then Congressman Dennis Hastert, who had once been a high school wrestling coach. The reaction of the convention delegates was mixed. Some disliked professional wrestling and wanted nothing to do with it or its members. Others felt that the Rock's introduction of Hastert was positive, and they welcomed his support.

THE FEUDS CONTINUE

Television, film, and politics were, for the moment, simply sidelines for Dwayne. Wrestling remained his main focus.

In the year 2000, the Rock continued his feud with Triple H and the McMahons. He won back the World Championship title but lost it again in October to Kurt Angle. He also won additional tag team championships, partnered with Mankind.

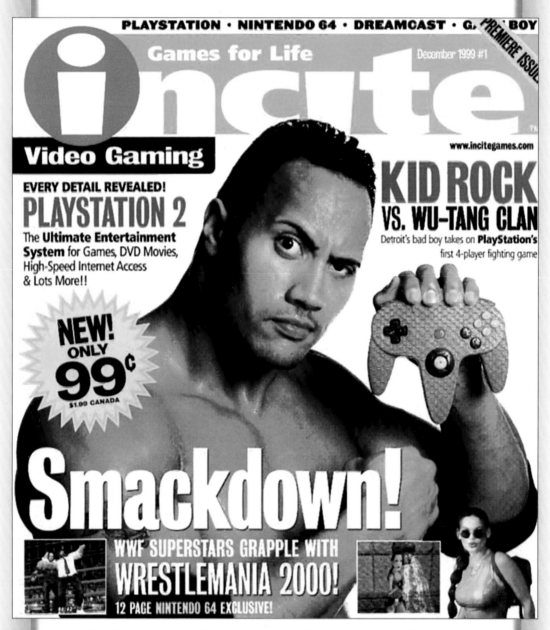

PLAYSTATION • NINTENDO 64 • DREAMCAST • G. BOY PREMIERE ISSUE

Games for Life

incite

December 1999 #1

Video Gaming

www.incitegames.com

EVERY DETAIL REVEALED!
PLAYSTATION 2
The **Ultimate Entertainment System** for Games, DVD Movies, High-Speed Internet Access & Lots More!!

KID ROCK
VS. WU-TANG CLAN
Detroit's bad boy takes on **PlayStation's** first 4-player fighting game

NEW!
ONLY
99¢
$1.99 CANADA

Smackdown!
WWF SUPERSTARS GRAPPLE WITH
WRESTLEMANIA 2000!
12 PAGE NINTENDO 64 EXCLUSIVE!

By the late 1990s, the Rock had become one of the most recognizable pro wrestlers. His picture appeared on the cover of many magazines, and he was invited to take part in television programs like *Saturday Night Live*. As his fame grew, Dwayne was offered the chance to start a new career as a movie actor.

In early 2001 the Rock won the World Championship title back from Angle. He then renewed his feud with Stone Cold Steve Austin. The two met in March at WrestleMania 17. Two years earlier, Mr. McMahon had helped the Rock, but this time he sided with Stone Cold. The two men finally pinned the Rock to end the match and to give Stone Cold the World Championship title.

Even in defeat, the Rock remained a fan favorite. Dwayne Johnson was at the height of his wrestling fame. He would continue wrestling for two more years, but he was about to find new fame as a movie star.

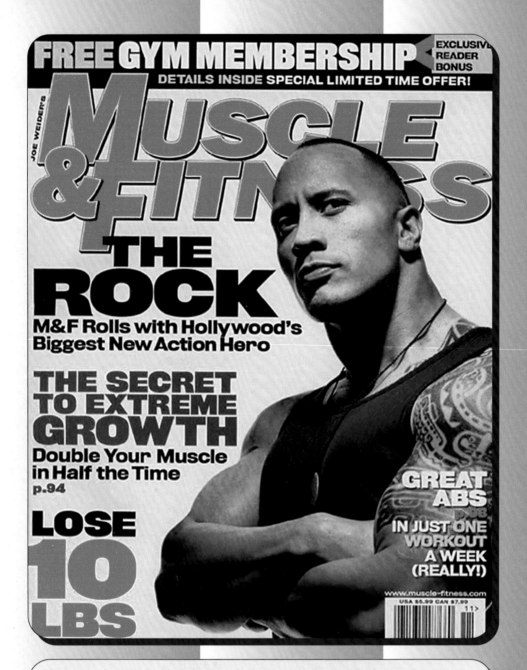

JOE WEIDER's

MUSCLE & FITNESS

THE ROCK

M&F Rolls with Hollywood's Biggest New Action Hero

THE SECRET TO EXTREME GROWTH

Double Your Muscle in Half the Time
p.94

LOSE 10 LBS

GREAT ABS
p.98
IN JUST ONE WORKOUT A WEEK (REALLY!)

www.muscle-fitness.com

USA $5.99 CAN $7.99

11>

Muscle & Fitness magazine calls the Rock "Hollywood's Biggest New Action Hero." As Dwayne moved from wrestling to movies, he knew that he would need to work hard to succeed. "I want the audience, and Hollywood, to know that I don't want to be considered [as] a celebrity who does a couple of movies," he has said. "I want to eventually, hopefully, become a decent actor who works with good actors."

5

The Rock as Movie Star

FOR DWAYNE JOHNSON, 2001 WAS AN IMPORTANT year. He and Dany became parents with the birth of their daughter, Simone Alexandra, on August 14. Dwayne also finally broke into the movies with *The Mummy Returns*. His role in that movie resulted in his first film lead, the title character of *The Scorpion King* (2002).

⇒ THE SCORPION KING ⇐

In *The Mummy Returns* Dwayne plays Mathayus, a king of ancient Egypt. Mathayus has made a deal with the Egyptian god **Anubis** for help in defeating the king's enemies. As part of the deal, Mathayus is changed into a half-man, half-scorpion and put to sleep for 5,000 years. In the 1930s a band of adventurers awakens him, and after a fierce battle, they manage to destroy Mathayus. The role was not large, and Dwayne had no spoken lines, but he impressed enough

DWAYNE "THE ROCK" JOHNSON

A scene from *The Scorpion King*, Dwayne's first major film role. Dwayne played a warrior who becomes king of ancient Egypt. The success of *The Scorpion King* proved that Dwayne made a good action hero. The movie earned more than $90 million in the United States, and over $164 million worldwide.

people to be offered the starring role in *The Scorpion King*. This film tells the story of Mathayus's early life.

Mathayus has much in common with the Rock. He is athletic, funny, and difficult to stop. In one early scene he is buried up to his neck in sand and must fight off attacks by scorpions with his teeth. Later, he is stung by a very deadly scorpion, and later still, shot with an arrow. None of these obstacles or any other dangers stop him from finally killing the villain and winning the heroine.

⇒ TAKING RISKS ⇐

Dwayne was pleased that a new career was opening up for him. Still, he knew there were risks in acting. Such a move was a gamble, yet he felt he had learned much about acting from wrestling. In a 2007 interview for the Australian newspaper *Herald Sun*, he remarked:

> **❝Wrestling's very over the top and theatrical—it was my theatre of 20,000 to 30,000 people. The audience will let you know how you're doing with your monologue, with your comedy. Your jokes, if they bomb, you know right away.❞**

Dwayne's gamble appeared to have paid off. True, critics were not excited about his acting in *The Scorpion King*. However, audiences enjoyed his performance and the film. The movie earned a respectable $90 million.

⇒ THE INVASION ⇐

Filming of *The Scorpion King* took most of the spring of 2001. During this time the Rock was absent from the ring. Mr. McMahon had supposedly suspended him.

In late July the Rock returned. Mr. McMahon had lifted the suspension because the WWE was in trouble. A rival organization, World Championship Wrestling (WCW), was mounting an invasion. The WCW's goal was to take over the WWE.

In reality the WWE had bought the WCW, and the WWE writers saw the takeover as a golden opportunity for an interesting new storyline. According to the storyline, some WWE wrestlers such as Stone Cold Steve Austin had joined the WCW invaders. Others remained loyal and opposed the WCW. In the end the Rock led the WWE team to victory over its rivals.

⟫ TAKING ON HULK HOGAN ⟪

In 2002 the Rock began a feud with Hulk Hogan. Hogan had been a legendary superstar in the 1980s and had recently returned to wrestling as a heel. The Rock and Hogan met at WrestleMania 18. The Rock won, but the crowd was clearly on Hogan's side. Heel or not, Hulk Hogan was even more popular than the Rock.

CROSS-CURRENTS

To find out about an unusual honor that Dwayne received in 2002, check out "The Rock in Wax." Go to page 56. ▶▶

In July 2002 the Rock won his seventh and final WWE World Championship title against Kurt Angle. A month later, the Rock lost the title to newcomer Brock Lesnar.

Unlike some wrestling stars, Dwayne never had a problem with letting the Rock lose to lesser-known wrestlers. To him, such losses were part of the business, and he regarded new blood as good for wrestling in general.

⟫ THE END OF WRESTLING ⟪

In 2003 the Rock's new gimmick was to bring a guitar into the ring and sing songs. These songs always insulted the host city of the WWE event. He also turned heel for the final time. In February he again met and defeated Hulk Hogan at the WWE event No Way Out. He also fought and defeated Stone Cold Steve Austin at WrestleMania 19. This was the last time the two rivals would meet in the ring.

The Rock continued to wrestle through 2003 and into 2004. By this time, however, Dwayne had decided his future lay in movies. He did not officially announce the Rock's retirement, but the Rock's final match was at WrestleMania 20 on March 12, 2004. Dwayne's contract with the WWE, and his wrestling career, ended on December 31, 2004.

⟫ ACTION HERO ⟪

As his wrestling career wound down, Dwayne followed up his role in *The Scorpion King* with a series of action-adventure movies. Dwayne's second starring role was as a **bounty hunter** named Beck in *The Rundown* (2003). In the movie, Beck goes to the Amazon to

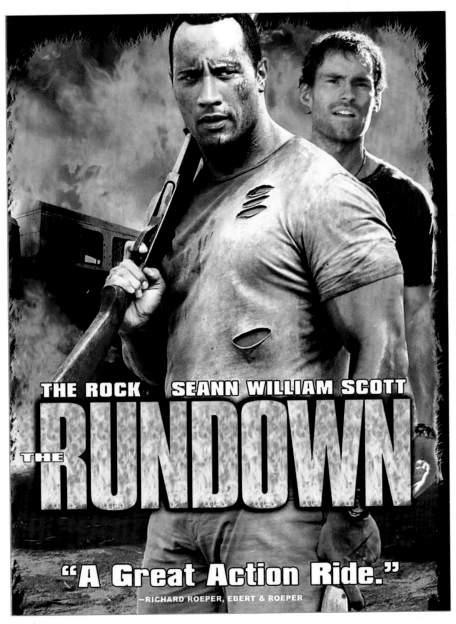

THE ROCK   SEANN WILLIAM SCOTT

THE RUNDOWN

"A Great Action Ride."
—RICHARD ROEPER, EBERT & ROEPER

Dwayne stayed in the action film genre with *The Rundown*, which also starred Seann William Scott. In the 2003 movie, Dwayne plays a bounty hunter who must rescue his employer's son (Scott) from the Amazon rainforest. The film received mostly good reviews from movie critics, and was a modest hit at the box office.

bring home a gangster's archeologist son to pay off a debt. There, Beck finds enemies, friends, treasure, and lots of action.

In 2004 Dwayne played Chris Vaughn in *Walking Tall*. Vaughn is a Special Forces veteran who uses his fighting skills—and a large piece of lumber—to clean up his hometown. The movie was full of high-energy action.

In 2005 Dwayne appeared in a film adaptation of the popular computer game *Doom*. As tough guy Sarge, he leads a group of Marines to destroy the monsters that have taken over a research station on Mars. Dwayne's character ends up becoming one of the monsters, and at the movie's end, he and the film's hero have a final fight, which Sarge loses.

None of these movies were very successful at the box office. The best earned about half of what *The Scorpion King* had. But Dwayne pleased audiences, and even critics admitted that he had a forceful screen presence.

⇒ NEW DIRECTIONS ⇐

In 2004, and between films, Dwayne visited Samoa for the first time since he was a child. He thought it would be a quiet vacation. Instead he found 30,000 people waiting at the airport to greet the Rock. His fame and that of his wrestling family were widespread among the islands. During his visit, Samoa's King Malietoa Tanumafili II made him a *seiuli*, a member of the Samoan nobility.

By 2005 Dwayne had a modest reputation as a rising action star. But he wanted to stretch himself by playing different kinds of roles. In 2005 he played a gay Samoan bodyguard in the John Travolta movie *Be Cool* and in 2007 starred as a down-on-his-luck actor in *Southland Tales*. In 2006, he was cast as a juvenile detention officer in *Gridiron Gang*. In that film his character, Sean Potter, does not go after street gangs with gun and fist. Rather, he forms a football team to help gang members find a crime-free life.

For the first time in his movie career, Dwayne's screen credit for *Southland Tales* was Dwayne Johnson, not the Rock. Dwayne had decided to retire the Rock name. In a 2006 story in the online gossip magazine *Expo Say*, he said:

"From now on please call me Dwayne Johnson. I want to be known as Dwayne Johnson the actor,

and not The Rock. I loved The Rock; The Rock was a nickname but what's happened is it's naturally progressed into Dwayne 'The Rock' Johnson. When it becomes just Dwayne Johnson, as it will in the next movie *Southland Tales*, that's fine. **"**

➤ A HELPING HAND ◀

Movies and wrestling have given Dwayne a public platform, which he uses to help others. In 2006, in addition to setting up the DJ Rock

The 2005 movie *Doom* was based on a popular video game. Dwayne played a tough marine sergeant who leads a team of soldiers fighting a horde of evil mutants. The film was extremely violent, and many movie critics did not like it. The movie only made about $28 million in the United States—half what it had cost to make.

Dwayne Johnson appeared with Mandy Moore in the 2007 film *Southland Tales*. The dramatic film about life in the United States after the start of the Third World War offered an opportunity for Dwayne to show his acting ability in a non-action role. However, the movie was a disappointment at the box office.

Foundation, he and his wife Dany gave the University of Miami $2 million. This money went toward rebuilding the university's **alumni** center. A year later, Dwayne and Dany gave the University of Miami another $1 million. This money went towards fixing up the football facilities. The donation was the largest ever given to the university's athletic department. In recognition of this generosity, the university renamed the football locker room in Dwayne's honor.

Dwayne has also given generous support to various Samoan organizations. He donates money to the Mapuifagalele Home for the Aged. He also is an active supporter of the Samoan **rugby** team. In 2007, during the Rugby World Cup, the team presented him with a team jersey with his name on the back.

⇛ SEPARATION FROM DANY ⇚

Dwayne has always kept his personal life as private as possible. Details of his home life and whatever strains his wrestling and acting have had on his marriage have mostly remained hidden. However, in June 2007, Dwayne and Dany announced that they were separating, but that they will remain friends. In addition, Dany will remain Dwayne's business partner in efforts such as the Rock Foundation.

⇛ A COMIC TURN ⇚

Dwayne's personal problems did not keep him idle. In 2007 his first comedy, *The Game Plan*, opened. Dwayne plays self-centered,

A scene from *The Game Plan*, in which Dwayne starred as a football player who suddenly learns he has an eight-year-old daughter. The Disney movie, which also starred Madison Pettis, Kyra Sedgwick, and Roselyn Sanchez, was a big hit. It was the number-one film in America for two straight weeks, and earned more than $90 million.

Dwayne Johnson has established himself as a popular entertainer through hard work and a willingness to take risks. "I would rather fail being aggressive than being passive and not trying to control what I can do," he says. "Because you know, I failed plenty of times, but if I [try hard], at least I'll feel like I'm doing something."

conceited professional quarterback Joe Kingman, who discovers he has an eight-year-old daughter. After first having a hard time accepting that fact, he eventually realizes how important she is to him. Dwayne brought something of his own relationship with his daughter to *The Game Plan*. In a 2008 interview with the British *Sun* he said:

> **"Fatherhood was difficult for me at first. . . . A lot of the time fathers struggle and I was one of those struggling dads. But if you are putting in the effort you are going to learn how to be a dad."**

The Game Plan did well. It was number one at the box office for its first two weeks and to date has earned over $90 million.

⇒ 2008 AND BEYOND ⇐

In 2008 Dwayne returned briefly to wrestling. On March 29 he spoke at the ceremony inducting his father, Rocky Johnson, and grandfather, Peter Maivia, into the WWE Hall of Fame. For a brief moment the Rock was back on stage.

But his focus now was on movies. In 2008 he appeared in a film based on the 1960s television spy spoof *Get Smart*, and lent his voice to the animated science fiction adventure *Planet 51*.

In the years to come, his fans, both new and old, can look forward to more movies. If there is one thing that Dwayne Johnson has proven throughout his career, it's that he knows how to entertain.

Children's Fitness Challenge

From its beginning the Rock Foundation has been a partner of the Children's Fitness Challenge. The Children's Fitness Challenge sponsors a series of athletic events around the country. In each event kids run an obstacle course. Each course is different and each has its own layout of obstacles. The course is 100 yards, and each child has to climb nets, jump hurdles, weave through a field of traffic cones, and slip under a low bar in order to reach the finish line. Despite these obstacles, the course is never so tricky that only very good athletes can complete it.

The first goal of the Children's Fitness Challenge is to promote exercise, healthy eating, and healthy living. There is also a second and larger goal. It seeks to promote children's self-esteem. By completing the course, children learn that they can overcome obstacles through hard work and discipline. Both the Children's Fitness Challenge and the Rock Foundation are confident that children will see that the effort used on the obstacle course is the same

Dwayne Johnson watches as his daughter Simone runs a Children's Fitness Challenge obstacle course. The goal of the nonprofit organization Children's Fitness Challenge is to encourage better health and fitness in young people. Dwayne's DJ Rock Foundation often partners with the Children's Fitness Challenge to sponsor events in American cities.

effort that will help them overcome the obstacles of life. For this reason, in the Children's Fitness Challenge, any child who finishes is a winner, and all who run the full course are given a certificate of victory.

(Go back to page 8.)

Samoa

The family of Dwayne "The Rock" Johnson's mother comes from the Samoan islands. These islands are in the South Pacific, about midway between Australia and Hawaii.

The Samoan islands are divided into two parts. The western part is the Independent State of Samoa, or Western Samoa, and the eastern is American Samoa. Western Samoa is an independent country with a land area of about 1,000 square miles and a population of about 217,000. American Samoa is a U.S. territory and has a land area of about 200 square miles and a population of around 57,000. The Maivia family comes from the Independent State of Samoa. Many people from both Western and American Samoa emigrate to the United States.

Polynesian seafarers first settled the Samoan islands some 3,000 years ago. In 1768 French explorers were the first Europeans to reach the islands. In 1899 the United States, Great Britain, and Germany took control of the islands. In 1962 Western Samoa gained its independence.

Traditional culture remains strong in both Samoas. For example, Samoans welcome visitors with a drinking ceremony known as the 'ava ceremony. Also, strict rules control the way people speak to and behave toward each other.

Samoans make their living by fishing and farming. There are also some factories that turn out clothes, shoes, and canned fruits and juices. Tourism is also big business.

(Go back to page 11.)

A Samoan crew paddles past modern buildings in a traditional longboat. Modern Samoans are descended from people who, over the course of many generations, rowed or sailed their small boats over vast distances. These people, known as Polynesians, settled on thousands of islands in the Pacific Ocean. Today, more than 217,000 people live in the Independent State of Samoa.

Rocky Johnson

Dwayne "The Rock" Johnson's father, Rocky Johnson, was born in Amherst, Nova Scotia, Canada, on August 24, 1944. (His real name was Wayde Bowles.) He trained first as a boxer and then in 1966 became one of the first African Americans in professional wrestling.

Before Rocky's first professional match, he trained with High Chief Peter Maivia, his future father-in-law and grandfather of the Rock. During his wrestling career, Rocky was known as the Soulman.

Rocky "Soulman" Johnson holds up the tag team championship belt he won with partner Tony Atlas in 1983. Dwayne's father was a highly regarded pro wrestler during the 1970s and early 1980s. In 2008, Rocky Johnson was inducted into the WWE Hall of Fame, along with Dwayne's grandfather, Peter "High Chief" Maivia.

Fighting Racism

In the 1960s it was not always easy being an African American wrestler. Wrestling was still mostly a sport for white men, and Rocky had to fight racism. Some white wrestlers would not fight with him, and others did their best to make him look bad in the ring. Still others actually punched or kicked him. In pro wrestling fighters are only supposed to pretend to be hurting one another.

Rocky, however, refused to quit, and soon he became a favorite with many wrestling fans. His athletic ability made him a dynamic performer who pleased audiences. One of his signature moves was his dancing footwork similar to that used by the boxer Muhammad Ali. Fans loved this dance.

During his career Rocky won almost 30 championships. His career high point was his 1983 World Tag Team Championship win. His tag team partner was Tony Atlas, another African American. The two became known as the Soul Patrol.

Hall of Fame

Rocky retired from wrestling in 1991. His retirement did not keep him entirely out of wrestling or the ring, however. In 1997 during WrestleMania 13, he leaped into the ring to help his son. Rocky also briefly worked for the WWE as a trainer in 2003.

On March 29, 2008, along with the Rock's grandfather, Peter Maivia, Rocky Johnson was inducted into the World Wrestling Entertainment Hall of Fame. According to the WWE Web page on Rocky:

"To some, he's known for being one of the greatest Superstars in WWE history; to others, he's known for being the son-in-law of the famed High Chief or the father of The Rock. However, as a pioneer and the first African-American to win coveted World Tag Team gold, Rocky Johnson will always be known as a legend and a trailblazer."

(Go back to page 14.)

Babyfaces and Heels

Like all good stories, wrestling storylines need good guys and bad guys. In wrestling, the good guys—the heroes—are babyfaces, also known as faces. The bad guys are heels, or villains. *Heel* is slang for a disgraceful and distasteful person. This term was commonly used in the United States throughout the first half of the twentieth century.

A babyface normally wins by being a good wrestler. He plays by the rules and wins through his skillful use of wrestling moves. A heel, however, wins by cheating. He may pick up a chair and hit the babyface, or he may call in another heel to help him.

Wrestling audiences are supposed to cheer the babyface and boo the heel. Sometimes, a heel becomes a crowd favorite, and he will then become a face.

Such a turnaround happened to both the Rock and Stone Cold Steve Austin. Often a heel turned face will keep many of his heel characteristics. The Rock continued to be boastful and self-centered as a face, and Stone Cold continued to curse and drink beer in the ring. Both occasionally resorted to tricks to win.

Indeed, since the mid-1990s many babyfaces have taken on characteristics once held only by heels. Modern wrestling audiences find such faces more colorful and fun. The older, clean-cut babyface now bores wrestling fans.

(Go back to page 18.)

Stone Cold Steve Austin

The Rock feuded with several wrestling greats during his career. His most famous feud was with Stone Cold Steve Austin. Like the Rock, Stone Cold was a WWE superstar and a fan favorite. During his career he held the WWE World Championship title six times and won three Royal Rumbles.

From Football to Wrestling

Steve Austin was born on December 18, 1964. In high school he was on the football, baseball, and track teams. He also had excellent grades and was a member of the National Honor Society. His football ability and his grades earned him a scholarship to North Texas State University.

After college, Steve attended wrestling school and in 1989 joined World Class Championship Wrestling. Two years later, he moved to World Championship Wrestling (WCW) and became Stunning Steve Austin. He was moderately successful, but never caught on big with the fans. In 1995 the WCW fired him after he was injured.

The Birth of Stone Cold

Late in 1995 Steve joined the WWE. He soon developed his Stone Cold character. As Stone Cold he was a trash-talking, bald-headed, beer-drinking heel with plenty of attitude. Stone Cold was an instant hit with the fans, and he soon turned from heel to babyface.

Stone Cold's signature move was the Stone Cold Stunner. Stone Cold would begin the move with a kick to his opponent's stomach. Then he would grab the other's head with both hands and fall backward. The trapped man would crash face first into the mat and be stunned. The Stone Cold Stunner usually ended a match with an Austin victory.

Feuding

Stone Cold's first major WWE feud was in 1997 with Bret and Owen Hart. During a match with Owen in the summer of that year, Stone Cold suffered a neck injury that almost ended his career. He returned late in 1997 for the first of his encounters with the Rock.

One of Stone Cold's most famous feuds was with Vince McMahon. McMahon was the head of WWE, but he also wrestled as Mr. McMahon. As a heel Mr. McMahon tried constantly but unsuccessfully to destroy Stone Cold's career.

Retirement

In 2003 Steve Austin retired as a full-time wrestler. He, did, however, continue to appear from time to time. Often, he would suddenly run into the ring and throw some wrestler down with the Stone Cold Stunner.

Like the Rock, Steve Austin also sought a new career in the movies. In 2007 he had his first starring role, in *The Condemned*.

(Go back to page 22.) ◀◀

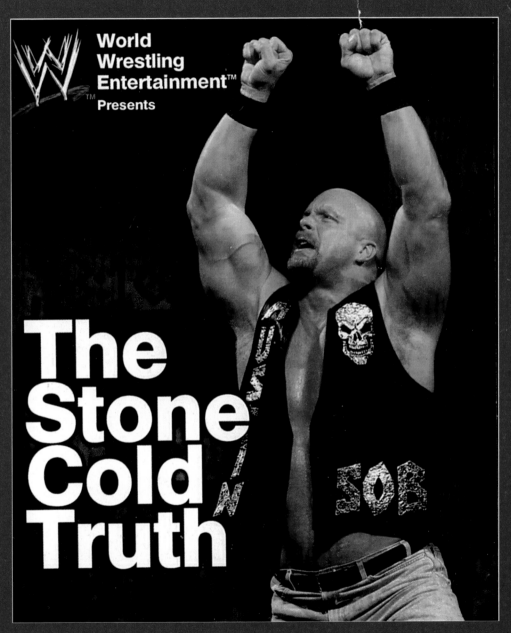

World Wrestling Entertainment™ Presents

The Stone Cold Truth

Steve Austin published his autobiography, The Stone Cold Truth, in 2003. In addition to the book, a DVD was produced that included interviews with the wrestler and footage from some of his greatest matches. Stone Cold Steve Austin was one of the most popular champions in WWE history. During his career, Stone Cold waged several memorable battles with the Rock.

Wrestling as Theater

Dwayne Johnson always speaks of professional wrestling as sports entertainment. He never calls pro wrestling simply a sport. It is not. In a true athletic contest, ability and skill lead to victory. In pro wrestling a script says who wins and who loses.

All wrestling organizations like World Wrestling Entertainment have a staff of writers. The writers turn out the scripts for matches, and they create the storylines that either throw various wrestlers together as partners or pit them against each other in feuds.

The wrestlers themselves are actors who do their own stunts. Each wrestler plays someone other than himself. The WWE writers come up with the various characters—Mankind, the Undertaker, and even the Rock. As good actors do, a star wrestler fleshes out his character. For Dwayne Johnson, he took the Rock and invented much of the character himself.

The wrestlers are not the only actors in wrestling. So are the referees and announcers. Indeed, a number of WWE people act as both referees and wrestlers.

Wrestling is a work of fiction. Everyone, including the audience, knows this. But this does not make the experience any less

High-flying aerial moves like this always impress fans at wrestling matches. Professional wrestlers often wear colorful costumes and dazzle audiences with their highly choreographed stunts. As a result, pro wrestling has become one of America's most popular forms of entertainment. Each week, wrestling shows on television attract more than 15 million viewers.

enjoyable for the fans. To them a pro wrestling match is just like a good action movie or TV show. It is fun to watch the antics of the wrestling greats and not-so-greats.

(Go back to page 28.)

The Rock Prepares for a Match

All professional wrestlers work from a script, but with stars such as the Rock, the writers often leave many of the details up to the wrestlers themselves. To prepare for WrestleMania 15, Dwayne Johnson and Steve Austin spent time working out their routine and then practicing it.

Working out the Routine

In the weeks before WrestleMania 15, the two men threw ideas at each other about the upcoming match. Both knew that the Rock was to lose to Stone Cold. They also knew that the match would last about 40 minutes. How they would fill those minutes and how they would fight each other was up to them.

Dwayne was confident that they would deliver a great show. He wrote in his auto-biography, *The Rock Says . . .*:

> **"I'd worked so often and so well with Steve in the past. I trusted him and he trusted me. We were a team, and there was no way we weren't going to put on one hell of a show."**

The morning of the match, Dwayne and Steve got together in the ring. They worked out their various moves. Among other things, they decided that real crowd pleasers would be for the Rock to fight free of Stone Cold's signature move, the Stone Cold Stunner, and for Stone Cold to do the same for the Rock's Rock Bottom. Dwayne and Steve were sure the fans would be delighted by these unexpected moves.

The two men met a second time in the afternoon to practice the match. They then decided how to work the referee into the match. Stone Cold was to hit him with a chair meant for the Rock.

The Bout

Dwayne's next task was to pump up the audience. The Rock gave an interview before the match in front of the crowd. In keeping with the Rock's image, Dwayne wore his most expensive clothes for the promo.

After the promo and just before the match, Dwayne and Steve met for a final time. They went over the entire routine and refined some of the details. Then both men changed into their ring gear.

The bout itself went off just as planned. As Dwayne and Steve hoped, the crowd went wild over the surprises during the match and the energy of the performance.

(Go back to page 30.)

The Rock in Wax

On April 10, 2002, the Madame Tussauds wax museum in New York unveiled the latest addition to its collection—the Rock. The Rock himself was on hand at the opening and entertained the crowd by posing for photographs in front of his life-sized wax figure. At one point he even kissed the wax statue.

The Madame Tussauds museums contain the most famous wax displays in the world. Originally, there was only one museum, in London, built by Marie Tussaud in the early nineteenth century. Tussaud had begun making life-sized wax figures in the 1770s. Her first figures included such eighteenth-century notables as Benjamin Franklin and the French writer, Voltaire.

The most popular attraction of the London museum is the Chamber of Horrors. It is filled with the statues of infamous murderers and other criminals. It also contains images of victims executed during the French Revolution.

In addition to the London museum, there are now six other Madame Tussauds around the world—in Amsterdam, Hong Kong, Shanghai, New York, Las Vegas, and Washington, D.C. The museum in New York has around 200 figures. Among them are such celebrities as Simon Cowell, Jennifer Lopez, Lindsay Lohan, Brad Pitt, and of course, the Rock.

A wax sculpture of Dwayne "The Rock" Johnson at Madame Tussauds wax museum in London, England. Being immortalized at Madame Tussauds is a sign that a celebrity has made it to the big time. Wax sculptures of Dwayne are also shown at the Madame Tussauds wax museums in New York and Las Vegas.

(Go back to page 40.) ◀◀

1972 Dwayne Douglas Johnson is born on May 2 in Hayward, California.

1991 Dwayne plays on the University of Miami's NCAA national football championship team.

1995 Dwayne joins the Canadian Football League's Calgary Stampeders but is dropped by the team after only a few months.

1996 Dwayne joins World Wrestling Entertainment in May. In November, as Rocky Maivia, he wins the WWE Survivor Series.

1997 In February Dwayne wins his first wrestling championship, and holds the Intercontinental Championship title. In May he marries Dany Garcia. He then joins the wrestling team the Nation of Dominance, takes on the name the Rock, and begins a long feud with Stone Cold Steve Austin.

1998 In November the Rock wins his first WWE Championship.

1999 The Rock plays his father, Rocky Johnson, on *That '70s Show*. In August he teams with Mankind as the Rock 'N' Sock Connection to win his first World Tag Team Championship.

2000 The Rock hosts *Saturday Night Live*. The Rock once more wins the WWE Championship and then loses it to Kurt Angle.

2001 The Rock films his first movie, *The Mummy Returns*. On August 14 his daughter, Simone Alexandra, is born.

2002 The Rock has his first leading film role in *The Scorpion King*. In the ring, he begins a feud with Hulk Hogan and defeats Hogan at WrestleMania 18.

2003 The Rock defeats Hulk Hogan a second and final time. In *The Rundown*, he has his second leading film role.

2004 The Rock has his last WWE match in March at WrestleMania 20. He stars in the movie *Walking Tall*.

2006 In September the Rock Foundation opens. Dwayne retires the name the Rock.

2007 Dwayne and his wife, Dany, announce their separation. He stars in his first comedy, *The Game Plan*.

2008 Dwayne helps induct his father, Rocky Johnson, and grandfather, Peter Maivia, into the WWE Hall of Fame. He has a role in *Get Smart*.

2009 Dwayne appears in the film *Race to Witch Mountain*.

Selected Awards

1988 All-conference (football), Lehigh Valley Conference

1991 Member of the University of Miami's NCAA National Championship football team

1997 Intercontinental Championship (wrestling)

1998 World Wrestling Entertainment Championship

1999 *Pro Wrestling Illustrated*'s Most Popular Wrestler of the Year
World Tag Team Championship
World Wrestling Entertainment Championship

2000 *Pro Wrestling Illustrated*'s Most Popular Wrestler of the Year
World Tag Team Championship
World Wrestling Entertainment Championship

2001 World Championship Wrestling Championship
Named by *E!* as one of the top 20 entertainers of the year
World Tag Team Championship
World Wrestling Entertainment Championship

2002 *Pro Wrestling Illustrated*'s Match of the Year
Nominated for Teen Choice Awards for Drama Action/Adventure Movie Actor
World Wrestling Entertainment Championship

2004 Nominated for MTV Movie Awards for the Best Fight
Nominated for Teen Choice Awards for Drama Action/Adventure Movie Actor

2006 Nominated for People's Choice Awards for Favorite Male Action Star

2007 *Wrestling Observer Newsletter* Hall of Fame

2008 Nominated for Kids' Choice Awards for Favorite Male Movie Star
Nominated for People's Choice Awards for Favorite Leading Man

Selected Films and TV

1999 *That '70s Show*

2000 *Star Trek: Voyager*
Saturday Night Live (host)

2001 *The Mummy Returns*

2002 *The Scorpion King*
Saturday Night Live (host)

2003 *The Rundown*

2004 *Walking Tall*

2005 *Be Cool*
Doom

2006 *Southland Tales*
Gridiron Gang

2007 *The Game Plan*

2008 *Get Smart*

2009 *Race to Witch Mountain*

Books

Hackett, Tomas. *Slaphappy: Pride, Prejudice, and Professional Wrestling*. New York: HarperCollins, 2006.

Johnson, Dwayne, with Joe Layden. *The Rock Says . . .* New York: HarperCollins, 2000.

Oliver, Greg, and Steven Johnson. *The Pro Wrestling Hall of Fame: The Heels*. Toronto: ECW Press, 2007.

———. *The Pro Wrestling Hall of Fame: The Tag Teams*. Toronto: ECW Press, 2005.

Pope, Kristian. *Tuff Stuff: Professional Wrestling Field Guide: Legend and Lore*. Iola, WI: KP Books, 2005.

Ross, Dan. *Pro Wrestling's Greatest Wars*. New York: Chelsea House, 2000.

Ross, Dan, Matt Hunter, and Kyle Alexander. *Pro Wrestling Legends*. New York: Chelsea House, 2005.

Web Sites

http://www.djrockfoundation.org/

The official Web site of the DJ Rock Foundation includes information on the organization's mission, history, and its various programs.

http://www.imdb.com/name/nm0425005/

Dwayne "The Rock" Johnson's page on the Internet Movie Database provides a listing of the Rock's wrestling events and films, his biography, and photographs, among other items.

http://www.wwe.com/superstars/halloffame/petermaivia/

This page from World Wrestling Entertainment provides a video, photographs, and a biography of the Rock's grandfather, Peter Maivia.

http://www.wwe.com/superstars/halloffame/rockyjohnson/

World Wrestling Entertainment's page for Rocky Johnson, the Rock's father, has a video, photographs, and a biography.

http://www.wwe.com/superstars/wwealumni/therock/

The Rock's page on the World Wrestling Entertainment's Web site has title listings, videos of matches, photographs, and a biography.

alumni—This word is used to refer to graduates or former students of a school, college, or university. Alumni is the plural form of alumna (a female graduate) or alumnus (a male graduate).

Anubis—the ancient Egyptian god of the dead. He had the body of a man and the head of a jackal, which is a relative of the wolf and the dog.

babyface—a hero, also known as a face, in the wrestling world.

body slam—when a wrestler picks up his opponent and throws him to the mat.

bounty hunter—a person not part of any law enforcement organizations who tracks down runaway criminals

choreograph—to map out the moves of wrestlers in the ring, in the wrestling world.

criminology—the study of crime and the ways of criminals.

forklift—a vehicle used to raise heavy boxes and other containers off the ground. The lift machinery is on the front of the vehicle; part of it looks like two large flat fingers.

heel—a villain, in the wrestling world.

ladder match—a bout in which two wrestlers try to beat each other to the top of a ladder; often one or both use the ladder as a weapon against the other.

leg drop—when a wrestler spins around in a circle on one leg and then drops his free leg onto the throat, chest, or stomach of a fallen opponent.

promo—a live or taped interview in which a wrestler brags about what he is going to do to an opponent.

rugby—a form of football which is popular outside the United States and in which two teams of 15 kick, pass, dribble, and run a ball down the field to score.

signature move—a move that a star wrestler has that is his and his alone. The Rock, for instance, has the People's Elbow and the Rock Bottom, and Stone Cold Steve Austin has the Stone Cold Stunner.

tag team—a team of two or more wrestlers who fight another team generally of equal number. Only one wrestler from each team is in the ring at a time, and a wrestler changes places with a teammate by touching, or tagging, him.

page 6 "By the beginning of 2000. . ." Thomas Chamberlin, "The Rock Greatness Parallel Roads to Triple H," *Wrestling Digest*, BNET (December 2000). http://findarticles.com/p/articles/mi_m0FCO/is_4_2/ai_67872116.

page 8 "Our staff and board of directors. . ." The DJ Rock Foundation (2008). http://www.djrockfoundation.org.

page 12 "I was fascinated. . ." Dwayne Johnson, with Joe Layden, *The Rock Says . . .* (New York: HarperCollins, 2000), p. 13–14.

page 15 "When Rocky Maivia. . ." Johnson, *The Rock Says . . .*, p. 206.

page 18 "Her parents were Cuban. . ." Zondra Hughes, "The Rock Talks About Race, Wrestling and Women," *Ebony* 100, no. 1 (June 18, 2001), p. 30.

page 19 "He is the kind . . ." "The Rock: Sexiest Wrestler," *People Weekly* 52, no. 19 (November 15, 1999), p. 84.

page 20 "I saw the Rock. . ." Johnson, *The Rock Says . . .*, pp. 226–227.

page 22 "There's nothing like working. . ." Scott B. Smith, "An Interview with The Rock," IGN.com (April 18, 2002). http://movies.ign.com/articles/357/357345p1.html.

page 27 "You know the outcome. . ." Grant Rollings, "Rock: I Call Dany My Sexy-exy," *Sun* (March 7, 2008). http://www.thesun.co.uk/sol/homepage/sport/wrestling/article890139.ece.

page 28 "We'll sit down. . ." "Dwayne 'The Rock' Johnson Discusses 'The Scorpion King,'" *CNN Larry King Weekend* (April 20, 2002). http://transcripts.cnn.com/TRANSCRIPTS/0204/20/lklw.01.html.

page 30 "Austin is getting the better. . ." Johnson, *The Rock Says . . .*, p. 348.

page 36 "I want the audience . . ." Steve Persall, "Rock Climbing," *The St. Petersburg (Florida) Times* (April 2, 2004), p. 1E.

page 39 "Wrestling's very over the top. . ." Claire Sutherland, "Dwayne 'The Rock' Johnson Checks In," *Herald Sun* (November 1, 2007). http://www.news.com.au/heraldsun/story/0,21985,22679430-5006023,00.html.

page 42 "From now on. . ." "'The Rock' Is out, Dwayne Johnson Is In," *Expo Say* (September 12, 2006). http://www.exposay.com/the-rock-is-out-dwayne-johnson-is-in/v/4288.

page 46 "I would rather fail . . ." Christine Spines, "Dwayne's World," *Entertainment Weekly* (June 13, 2008), p. 22.

page 47 "Fatherhood was difficult. . ." Rollings, "Rock: I Call Dany My Sexy-exy."

page 51 "To some, he's known. . ." "Rocky Johnson," World Wrestling Entertainment (2008). http://www.wwe.com/superstars/halloffame/rockyjohnson/bio.

page 55 "I'd worked so often. . ." Johnson, *The Rock Says . . .*, p. 330.

James A. Corrick has been a professional writer and editor for thirty years. Along with a PhD. in English, his academic background includes a graduate degree in the biological sciences. He has taught English, edited magazines for the National Space Society, and edited and indexed books on history, economics, and literature. Among his other books are *The Civil War*, *Life Among the Incas*, *The Early Middle Ages*, *The Renaissance*, and *The Civil War and Emancipation*. He and his wife live in Tucson, Arizona.

PICTURE CREDITS

page

1: Jeffrey Mayer/WireImage
4: Walt Disney/PRMS
7: Gregg DeGuire/WireImage
9: Fisher-Price/NMI
10: The Johnson Family/ASP Library
13: Getty Images
16: WWE/PRMS
19: Splash News
21: WWE/PRMS
24: Rich Freeda/WWE/PRMS
26: WWE/PRMS
29: WWE/PRMS
31: Rich Freeda/Titan Sports/KRT
34: New Millennium Images

36: Muscle & Fitness/NMI
38: Universal Pictures/NMI
41: Universal Pictures/NMI
43: Universal Pictures/NMI
44: Universal Pictures/NMI
45: Walt Disney Pictures/NMI
46: Man's Journal/NMI
48: The Rock Foundation/CIC Photos
49: T&T/IOA Photos
50: WWE/PRMS
53: WWE/NMI
54: WWE/PRMS
56: London Entertainment /Splash

Front cover: WWE/PRMS